CONTENTS

China and its Food

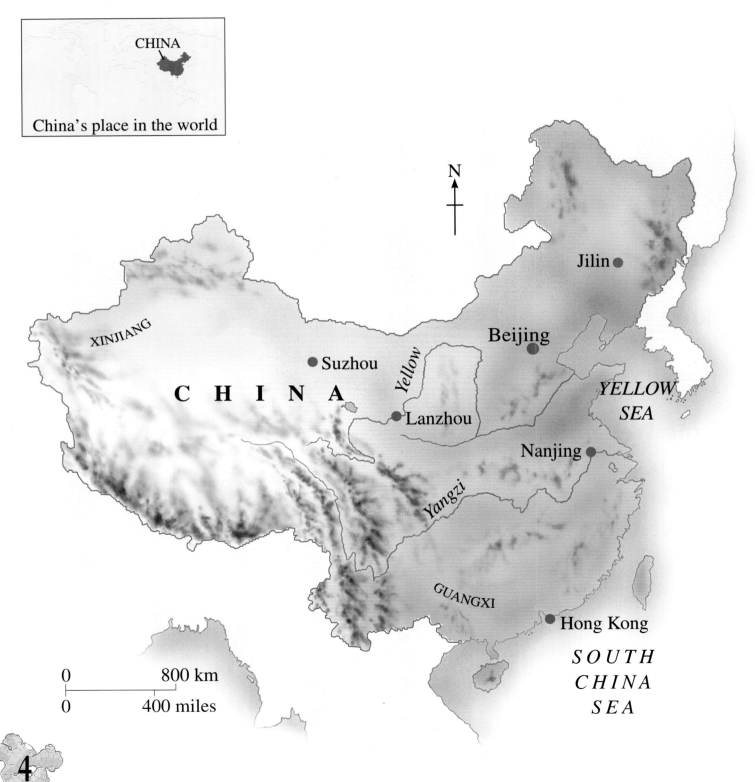

CHINA

China's place in the world

N

Jilin

Beijing

XINJIANG

Suzhou

C H I N A

Yellow

Lanzhou

YELLOW SEA

Nanjing

Yangzi

GUANGXI

Hong Kong

SOUTH CHINA SEA

| 0 | 800 km |
| 0 | 400 miles |

RICE

Rice is an important staple food, especially in southern China. It needs a warm climate and lots of water to grow.

NOODLES

Noodles are an important part of many Chinese meals. They are made from wheat, a staple food in northern China.

PORK

Pork is the favourite meat in much of China. In the past, many families kept a few pigs, which were killed to provide meat for festivals.

POULTRY

Hens, ducks and geese supply eggs and meat. One of China's most famous dishes is Peking Duck – slices of duck wrapped in a thin pancake.

SOYA BEANS

Soya beans are very nutritious and can be made into many different products, such as soya-bean milk, soy sauce and bean curd, or tofu.

VEGETABLES

A huge range of vegetables are grown, especially in southern China. Vegetables stir-fried for a short time in a very hot wok are tasty and full of nutrients.

Food and Farming

More people live in China than in any other country in the world – over 1.25 billion people. But China is not the world's largest country, and much of the land cannot be farmed because there are many mountains and some deserts. So for hundreds of years, China's farmers have had to work very hard to produce enough food for people to eat.

▼ Farm workers in Guangxi Province spread out rice to dry.

Farming in China is still very hard work. Most families in the countryside have farm land that is about the size of three football pitches. Often, this land is split up into several small plots.

Many people in China now live in cities, but most are from farming families, so they know how difficult it can be to produce enough food.

'HAVE YOU EATEN?'

In the past, many Chinese families have gone hungry during famines. That is why the Chinese way of saying 'Hello' or 'How are you?' is to ask 'Have you eaten?' The idea is that if you've had something to eat, then life must be all right for you.

▼ People enjoying a snack at a roadside stall in Lanzhou.

Growing rice

Chinese farmers have been growing rice for more than 3,000 years. It is a good way to provide a lot of food from a small area of land.

Rice needs a lot of water to grow. Rice fields have to be very flat, because they have to be 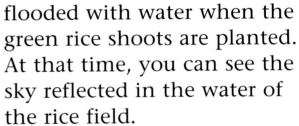 flooded with water when the green rice shoots are planted. At that time, you can see the sky reflected in the water of the rice field.

A few months later, the rice is ready for harvesting and the fields are almost dry. From a distance, it looks as if they are covered in a yellow blanket.

◀ A mother and her daughter harvesting rice in Guangxi Province.

Staple foods

Rice is not the only staple food in China. Wheat, millet and barley are important foods in the north. Wheat is made into noodles, steamed bread, or the wrappings for dumplings. In some parts of China, people sometimes eat sweet potatoes as their staple food.

Staple foods are the main part of everyday meals. But at festivals, people enjoy a rich variety of special foods, which are much tastier.

▲ Workers in north-west China winnowing wheat.

Making noodles in Xinjiang ▶ Province. Noodles are often served at birthday banquets, as a way of wishing people a long life.

Banquets

In China, births, marriages and business deals are all celebrated with banquets. Banquets are also held when someone dies.

Wealthy people spend a great deal of money on banquets. But for ordinary people, family events and festivals give them the opportunity to eat expensive meat and other special foods.

TASTY DISHES

In the past, large banquets were prepared for the Chinese emperors (kings). They included delicacies such as the lining of a swallow's nest, bear's paw, camel's hump, gorilla's lips, and deer's tail. Today in China, you can still try delicacies such as turtle, pig's ear, snake-meat, crab, sea slug and whole frogs.

◀ A bride and groom enjoy the banquet at their wedding in Jilin.

Gods, ghosts and ancestors

In the past, Chinese festivals were held in honour of the gods, ghosts and ancestors. Farmers thanked the gods and ancestors for the blessings of the past year, and prayed for peace and wealth in the year to come. The noise of exploding firecrackers would scare harmful ghosts away from the celebrations. Festivals gave farmers a chance to rest from their work, and to enjoy plenty of good food.

The main religions of China in the past were Buddhism, Taoism and Confucianism. Today, many Chinese people do not follow any religion – but they still enjoy the festivals!

▲ People in Beijing taking part in a colourful festival celebrating the story of the Monkey God.

Chinese New Year

The Chinese New Year festival is the most important family holiday of the year. It takes place near the end of January, or early in February, and it is also called the Spring Festival. It is a time to celebrate the 'death' of the old year, and the 'birth' of the new year. It is traditional for everyone in the family to get together to share the New Year's Eve feast.

THE STOVE GOD

In Chinese legend, the Stove God spies on each family from his place in the kitchen. A few days before the end of the year, he goes to the Heaven Emperor to report on the family's behaviour. Just before he leaves, the family offers him lots of sticky sweets, so that his teeth get stuck together. This is a trick, so that the Stove God either can't make his report, or can only say sweet things about the family.

▼ These geese are going to be sold for a New Year feast.

12

Preparing the feast

In the days before Chinese New Year, food shops and market stalls are very busy. In the north of China, families work hard together to make dozens, or even hundreds, of *jiaozi* for the New Year's Eve feast. *Jiaozi* are wrapped dumplings, usually filled with minced pork. People prepare too much food for the feast on purpose – the idea is that then there will be food left over for the year ahead.

When all the food is cooked, families offer it to their ancestors, first. Then it is the family's turn to eat.

◀ Making *Jiaozi* is fun when everyone in the family helps.

13

▲ Tables are crammed with tasty dishes for the New Year's Eve banquet.

How the festival began

There is a story about how the New Year festival started. Long ago, the Heaven Emperor sent a New Year monster to destroy the world because human beings were not looking after their animals properly. People were very frightened. They made a farewell meal to enjoy as a family, and waited through the dark night for the world to end.

Only when day came did they realize that the Heaven Emperor had forgiven them. They rushed outside to say 'congratulations' to all their friends and neighbours. People still greet each other in this way on New Year's Day.

This enormous puppet ▶ is performing a lion dance in Beijing, to welcome the New Year.

15

Favourite dishes

At the New Year's Eve banquet, there is usually one dish that is a whole fish, which stands for wholeness and prosperity. Foods that are round in shape (such as whole eggs or sweet riceballs) mean that families will be 'complete' and get on well with each other.

Sticky New Year cake, which is a sponge cake, is often included, because the word for 'cake' sounds the same as the Chinese word for 'tall' or 'high'. So eating cake is a way of wishing for success or promotion. There is a recipe for a Chinese sponge cake on the opposite page.

▼ Sticky cake and other New Year specialities are on sale in this shop.

Steamed Sponge Cake

INGREDIENTS

4 Eggs
120 g Sugar
1 Teaspoon of molasses
30 g Margarine
100 ml Milk

2 Tablespoons of vegetable oil
225 g Self-raising flour
½ Teaspoon of bicarbonate of soda

EQUIPMENT

Mixing bowl
Wooden spoon
Greased pudding bowl
Baking parchment
Piece of string
Large saucepan
Plate
Palette knife

Mix together the eggs, sugar, molasses and margarine. Mix in the milk and vegetable oil, then the flour and bicarbonate of soda.

Pour the cake mixture into the pudding bowl and tie a circle of baking parchment over the top. Quarter-fill the saucepan with water and stand the pudding bowl inside it.

Put the lid on the saucepan, leaving a little gap. Boil the water gently for 35–40 minutes. Carefully push a knife into the centre of the cake mixture – if it comes out dry, the cake is done.

Slide the palette knife around the inside of the bowl, then turn it upside-down on a plate to release the cake. Serve hot, with warmed clear honey, golden syrup or raspberry sauce.

Always be careful with hot pans. Ask an adult to help you.

Tomb-sweeping Festival

The Tomb-sweeping Festival (which is also called the Qing Ming Festival) takes place each year in early April. It is a time for families to show that they have not forgotten relatives who have died. They go to the tombs of their ancestors and clean weeds off the graves. Sometimes they light sticks of incense at the graveside. They might offer baskets of food and burn spirit money for their ancestors. They let off firecrackers, too.

Some families have a picnic at the graveside. Other families have a special meal at home, as a way of remembering their ancestors.

◄ These people have brought a picnic to a graveside for the Tomb-sweeping Festival in Hong Kong.

18

Remembering ancestors

It is important for families to take care of the spirits of their ancestors and make them comfortable in the world of the dead. According to tradition, ancestors who are not looked after by the living become ghosts. They have nowhere to stay, so they are wandering ghosts. They have no one to offer them food, so they are hungry ghosts. These ghosts may harm people in their efforts to get food and shelter.

GHOST MONTH

In the Chinese calendar, the seventh month is Ghost Month, when all the ghosts are released from Hell. At this time, people feel sorry for these souls who have no one to take care of them. They offer huge amounts of food and spirit money to ease the ghosts' suffering.

▼ These Chinese people are burning spirit money as an offering at a funeral.

New life

▼ These pancake rolls are called lucky egg rolls, or *ru yi dan juan*. They are filled with egg and thinly sliced vegetables, and cut into slices.

The Tomb-sweeping Festival also marks the time when seeds are planted. So it is a time for remembering the dead, and for celebrating new life. By celebrating these things together, people hope that the ancestors will bless the new crops that are being planted.

The foods eaten at the Tomb-sweeping Festival include pancake rolls filled with a mixture of ingredients. These stand for the togetherness of the family and their ancestors. There is a recipe for pancake rolls on the opposite page.

EGGS

Some families eat hard-boiled eggs at their graveside picnic. They throw the eggshells on top of the tomb. Eggs are a sign for life, death and life beginning again – like the Easter eggs of the Christian religion.

Pancake rolls

EQUIPMENT

Large bowl   Ladle
Wooden spoon or   Frying pan
electric food mixer   Spatula

INGREDIENTS

For the pancake batter
185 g Plain flour
½ Teaspoon of salt
2 eggs
375 ml of water
3 Tablespoons of Hoisin sauce

For the fillings (serve in small bowls)
Thinly-sliced stir-fried chicken,
  pork, or ham

Thinly-sliced stir-fried vegetables:
  carrots, celery, beansprouts,
  peppers, shitake mushrooms

1 Mix together the flour, salt and eggs. Blend in the water gradually to make a smooth batter.

2 Heat a lightly greased frying pan. Ladle in a little batter, turning the pan to spread the batter thinly and evenly.

3 Cook the pancake until it lifts off easily when you slide a spatula under it. Turn the pancake over to cook the other side.

4 Spread a little Hoisin sauce on the pancake. Place the filling of your choice in a line across the pancake and roll it up.

Always be careful with hot pans. Ask an adult to help you.

Dragon-boat Festival

The Dragon-boat Festival is held on the fifth day of the fifth lunar month, which is in May or June. On this day, for hundreds of years, teams of rowers have raced against each other in boats that are shaped like dragons.

The festival is held to honour an honest politician, who drowned himself when people ignored his advice about how to save China. According to the story, people raced in their boats to try to save him. Also, the dragon boats, which are rowed to the beat of drums, are supposed to frighten fish away, so that they will not feed on the dead body of the politician.

◀ A dragon boat races across Hong Kong harbour.

Zongzi

The most famous food for the Dragon-boat Festival is *zongzi*. These are sticky-rice dumplings, with a filling of either pork, or bean and egg, or sweet red-bean paste, all wrapped in bamboo leaves. They are about the size of a tennis ball, and are tied together with string.

According to the story, when the honest politician drowned himself, people threw *zongzi* into the lake. They did this so that the fish would eat the *zongzi* instead of the body of the drowned politician.

▼ *Zongzi* are sometimes given as gifts when people visit friends and relatives at festival time.

Dragons in the sky

The Dragon-boat Festival is also at the beginning of the summer, when the weather starts to get hot. It is the time when the crops should be ripening, and rain is needed for a good harvest. Some people think that the dragon-boat race is held to encourage the rain to fall. This is because in Chinese tradition, dragons fighting in the sky are thought to bring heavy rain.

BALANCING EGGS

The Dragon-boat Festival takes place close to the summer solstice, when the sun is directly overhead at noon. Some people say that at this time it is possible to balance an egg on its pointed end on level ground. Children have great fun trying to do this on their doorsteps. You might like to try this yourself. Or you can try to make tea eggs instead – there is a recipe on the opposite page.

Tea eggs on a bed ▶
of lettuce.

Tea Eggs

EQUIPMENT

Large saucepan
Large spoon

INGREDIENTS

6 Eggs
6 Tablespoons of soy sauce
2 Teabags
2 Teaspoons of salt
½ teaspoon of five-spice powder

The longer you leave the eggs in the tea liquid, the more the flavour will seep in and the stronger the marble pattern will be.

1 Put the eggs in the saucepan, cover them with water and simmer for about 10 minutes. Pour away the hot water and cover the eggs with cold water.

2 When the eggs are cool, pour away the water. Crack the shells all round without peeling off the eggshells.

3 Cover the cracked eggs with cold water and add the teabags, soy sauce, salt and five-spice powder. Simmer for an hour.

4 Leave the eggs to cool in the tea liquid. Then peel the eggs and serve them warm or cold, on shredded lettuce.

Always be careful with hot pans. Ask an adult to help you.

Moon Festival

The Moon Festival is also known as the Mid-Autumn Festival. This is the time when people admire the full moon for looking especially round and bright. In the past, the festival was a time for celebrating the harvest. Today, some parents let their children stay up late, and may take them to a park or hill-top to admire the moon and enjoy a picnic.

This woman is dressed as the Moon Princess.

MOON PRINCESS

The Moon Festival is thought of mainly as a festival for women to enjoy. In Chinese thinking, the moon is thought of as female, while the sun is thought of as male. A beautiful princess, called Chang E, is said to have been banished to the moon as a punishment. She took a pill that would have made her husband live for ever. On the day of the Moon Festival, she is at her most beautiful.

Festival fruits

A number of fruits are eaten at Moon Festival time. These include different sorts of citrus fruit, pomegranates, round pears and a fruit called carambola. All these fruits are round like the moon. People give fruits like these as gifts at Moon festival time so that families are 'round' or 'complete', too.

▲ Festive lanterns light up the night in a Hong Kong park.

Round fruits like ▶ these colourful pomegranates are eaten at the time of the Moon Festival.

Moon cakes

Moon cakes are the most famous foods at the Moon Festival. They are difficult to make, so people buy them from shops rather than making them at home. But they are expensive.

The round moon cakes have golden-brown pastry on the outside and all sorts of rich fillings on the inside. A mixture of ground lotus nuts or other nuts is quite popular. Some moon cakes have the yolk of a duck egg inside. They are very filling to eat. You wouldn't be able to manage more than one at a time.

▼ A shop owner prepares his display of moon cakes, ready for the festival.

CHINESE WRITING

To give you a flavour of Chinese writing, as well as Chinese eating, there is a recipe for round almond biscuits on the opposite page. You can write the Chinese word for 'moon' on them. This is how to write it:

Almond biscuits

EQUIPMENT

Large bowl
Wooden spoon
Baking tray
Pastry brush

Spatula
Cooling rack
Fine, clean
   paintbrush

INGREDIENTS

125 g Self-raising flour
1 Teaspoon baking powder
125 g Sugar
100 g Ground almonds
50 g Margarine
2 Eggs, beaten
Red food colouring

Mix together the flour, baking powder, sugar and ground almonds. Rub in the margarine with your fingers until the mixture is like breadcrumbs. Mix in one egg.

Divide the mixture into 12 portions. Roll each between your hands. Flatten it into a round shape. Put the shapes on a greased baking tray. Brush the tops with beaten egg.

Bake the biscuits at 200°C/Gas mark 6 for 20 minutes until they are golden brown. Lift them off the baking tray and leave them to cool on a rack.

Dip a clean, fine brush into the red food colouring and draw a round moon shape on the biscuit, or write the Chinese character for 'moon'.

Always be careful with hot pans. Ask an adult to help you.

Glossary

Ancestors   Family members who have died, usually a long time ago.

Banquet   A large feast.

Buddhism   A religion which was begun by the Buddha, who lived in northern India.

Confucianism   The ideas of the ancient chinese teacher Confucius. He taught about the importance of the family, and respect for parents.

Dumplings   Small balls of dough, with savoury fillings.

Famines   Times when people have no food, or very little food to eat.

Firecrackers   Fireworks that make a loud noise when they go off.

Incense   Sticks or powder that give off a sweet smell when they are burnt.

Lunar month   The period between one new moon and the next, which is just over 29 days. The dates of many Chinese festivals are worked out according to the movements of the moon, instead of being on a fixed date.

Noodles   A food made from flour and shaped into long, thin ribbons. They are a bit like spaghetti.

Nutritious   Full of nutrients, things that the body needs to stay healthy.

Staple foods   Foods that are the main part of people's everyday meals, such as rice, bread or potatoes.

Taoism (also spelt Daoism)   A Chinese way of thinking about what it means to be human, and how humans are part of nature and the universe.

Winnowing   Separating the grain from the stalks of plants by throwing it into the air. The stalks blow away and the grain, which is heavier, falls to the ground.

Topic Web and Resources

MATHS
Using and understanding data and measures (recipes).

Using and reading measuring instruments: scales.

Using weights and measures.

Using and understanding fractions.

SCIENCE
Food and nutrition.

Health.

Plants in different habitats.

Plants as a life process.

Separating mixtures of materials: sieving and dissolving.

Changing materials through heat.

GEOGRAPHY
Locality study.

Landscapes and climate.

Farming.

Influence of landscape on human activities: farming and food festivals.

Awareness of wider context of a place.

DESIGN AND TECHNOLOGY
Design a poster to advertise a food product.

Technology used in food production.

Packaging.

Food preparation.

Follow a recipe.

Festivals & Food TOPIC WEB

HISTORY
Migrations.

ENGLISH
Make up a slogan to sell a food product.

Write a poem or story using food as the subject.

Write a menu you might find in a Chinese restaurant.

RE
Festivals.

Buddhism.

Respect for ancestors.

Importance of families.

MODERN FOREIGN LANGUAGES
Language skills.

Everyday activities: food.

People, places and customs.

OTHER BOOKS TO READ

A World of Recipes: China by Julie McCulloch (Heinemann Library, 2002)

Celebrate! Chinese New Year by Mike Hirst (Hodder Wayland, 2002)

Country Insights: China by Julia Waterlow (Hodder Wayland, 2006)

Discover Other Cultures: Festivals Around The World by Meryl Doney (Franklin Watts, 2002)

Special Ceremonies: Feasts and Fasting by Cath Senker (Franklin Watts, 2005)

This book meets the following specific objectives of the National Literacy Strategy's Framework for Teaching:

✓ Range of work in non-fiction: simple recipes (especially Year 2, Term 1), instructions, labels, captions, lists, glossary, index.

✓ Vocabulary extension: words linked to particular topics (food words) and technical words from work in other subjects (geography and food science).

Index

Page numbers in **bold** mean there is a photograph on the page.